W9-ATK-367

Skills Practice

Grade K

Mc
Graw
Hill
Education

Bothell, WA • Chicago, IL • Columbus, OH • New York, NY

MHEonline.com

Send all inquiries to:
McGraw-Hill Education
8787 Orion Place
Columbus, OH 43240

ISBN: 978-0-07-668490-8
MHID: 0-07-668490-3

Printed in the United States of America.

5 6 7 8 9 10 LHS 20 19

Table of Contents

Unit 11

Unit 12

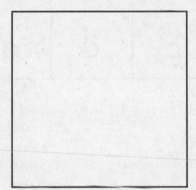

Directions: Draw a smiley face in each box just like the one pictured.

Name _____ **Date** _____

Directions: Color the boxes that have a C, c, D, or d. Use one color for C, c, and another color for D, d.

e	B	t	c	B	R
Y	M	D	H	b	C
B	b	E	C	M	d
c	d	a	F	D	g

C C D D

ions: Start at the large dot and follow the dotted line to each letter.

Alphabetic Knowledge • *Skills Practice*

Name ____________________ Date __________

E E D D

B B F F

H H K K

T T L L

Directions: Start at the large dot and follow the dotted line to complete each letter.

Directions: Color the boxes that have a *G*, *g*, *H*, or *h*. Use one color for *G*, *g*, and another color for *H*, *h*.

L	B	T	q	H	y
h	p	Y	g	b	C
B	H	G	o	M	g
Q	d	N	F	h	G

G G   H H

Directions: Start at the large dot and follow the dotted line to complete each letter.

Directions: Find and circle capital letters A, B, C, D, E, F, G, and H.

Directions: Find and circle lowercase letters *a, b, c, d, e, f, g,* and *h.*

Alphabetic Knowledge • *Skills Practice*

E E

Z Z

A A

F F

H H

G G

T T

L L

Directions: Start at the large dot and follow the dotted line to complete each letter.

Directions: Color the boxes that have a *K, k, L,* or *l.* Use one color
for *K, k,* and another color for *L, l.*

L	K	t	q	H	l
h	i	Y	L	b	C
k	H	l	o	K	I
Q	d	N	F	h	k

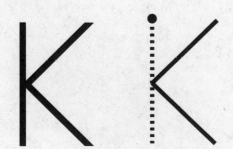

Directions: Start at the large dot and follow the dotted line to
complete each letter.

Alphabetic Knowledge • *Skills Practice*

E	M	a	B	h	n
Y	v	n	t	M	R
f	N	C	m	g	A
M	T	s	G	e	m
b	m	H	c	N	F
S	V	r	M	y	n

Directions: Color the boxes that have an M, m, N, or n. Use one color for M, m, and another color for N, n.

O  p

 p O

 b r

 R b

 o P

 B R

Directions: Find and circle letters *O*, *o*, *P*, and *p*.

Alphabetic Knowledge • *Skills Practice*

Directions: Connect the dots, in order from *A–P*, to complete the picture of the bluebird.

A A A   W W W

V V V   K K K

X X X   M M M

Directions: Start at the large dot and follow the dotted line to complete each letter.

Penmanship • *Skills Practice*

A A N N

V V W W

X X M M

Directions: Start at the large dot and follow the dotted line to complete each letter.

 S

 U

 t

s

 f

 W

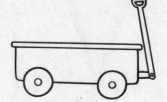

 u

T

I

Directions: Find and circle letters S, s, T, t, U, and u.

Alphabetic Knowledge • *Skills Practice*

A A N N

V V W W

X X M M

Directions: Start at the large dot and follow the dotted line to complete each letter.

Directions: Color the boxes that have an X, x, Y, y, Z, or z. Use
three different colors: one for X, x, one for Y, y, and one for Z, z.

Y	K	t	q	H	Z
H	Z	y	X	b	s
k	H	S	z	K	Y
x	d	z	F	h	k

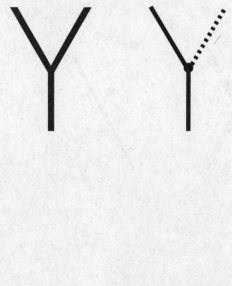

Directions: Start at the large dot and follow the dotted line to
complete each letter.

Alphabetic Knowledge • *Skills Practice*

Directions: Connect the dots in alphabetical order from *N* to *Z* to complete the picture of the willow tree.

D D   O O

B B   R R

P P   Q Q

p p   b b

Directions: Start at the large dot and follow the dotted line to complete each letter.

Penmanship • *Skills Practice*

C c  Q

G 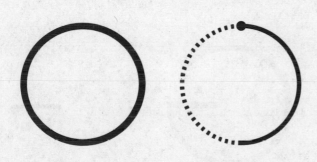 d

O 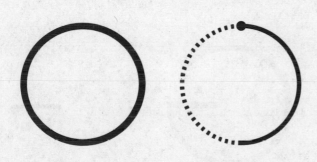 p

e g

Directions: Start at the large dot and follow the dotted line to complete each letter.

D D

B B

O O

R R

Q Q

G G

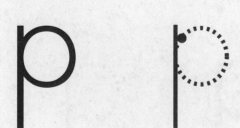

p p

e e

Directions: Start at the large dot and follow the dotted line to complete each letter.

Penmanship • *Skills Practice*

O O d

Q Q g

a  p p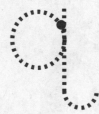

b b q q

Directions: Start at the large dot and follow the dotted line to complete each letter.

Q

B

D

S

F

P

p

s

f

b

q

d

Directions: Draw a line from the capital letter to its matching lowercase letter.

Name ________________________ Date ________

g g d d

a a O O

Q Q q q

p p b b

Directions: Start at the large dot and follow the dotted line to complete each letter.

Directions: Look at the number on the monkeys' shirts. Draw the correct number of circles inside each basket.

K K

L L

A A

F F

T T

D D

B B

P P

Directions: Start at the large dot and follow the dotted line to complete each letter.

Skills Practice • Penmanship

Tt	Nn	Ee	Ss

tens	sent
spin	mint
nets	pens
rest	nest

Directions: Circle the words that contain all the letters listed at the top of the page.

Alphabetic Knowledge • *Skills Practice*

A A   K

V V   X X

M M 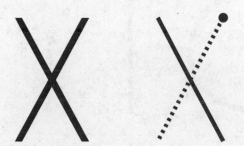   W W

Y Y   N N

Directions: Start at the large dot and follow the dotted line to complete each letter.

Skills Practice • Penmanship   UNIT 2 • Lesson 3 • Day 3 **27**

Name _____ **Date** _____

G G   B B

D D   C

Q Q   g

p p   b

Directions: Start at the large dot and follow the dotted line to complete each letter.

Penmanship • *Skills Practice*

Ss

S

s

Directions: Write the capital and lowercase forms of the letter Ss.
Write the letter s under the picture whose name begins with the /s/ sound.

S s

_____

- - - - - - - - - - - - - - - - - - -

_____

_____

- - - - - - - - - - - - - - - - - - -

_____

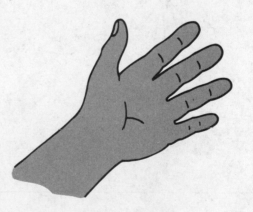

_____

- - - - - - - - - - - - - - - - - - -

_____

_____

- - - - - - - - - - - - - - - - - - -

_____

Directions: Write the letter s under each picture whose name begins with the /s/ sound.

Alphabetic Principle • *Skills Practice*

_____

- - - - - - - - - - - - - - - - -

_____

_____

- - - - - - - - - - - - - - - - -

_____

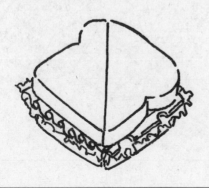

_____

- - - - - - - - - - - - - - - - -

_____

Directions: Write the letter s under each picture whose name ends with the /s/ sound.

Mm

M _____

m _____

_____

_____

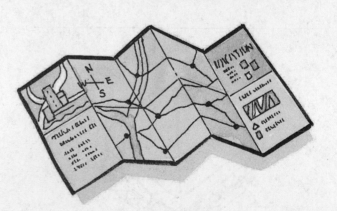

_____

_____

Directions: Write the capital and lowercase forms of the letter *Mm*. Write the letter *m* under the picture whose name begins with the /m/ sound.

_____

- - - - - - - - - - - - - - - - -

_____

_____

- - - - - - - - - - - - - - - - -

_____

Directions: Write the letter *m* under each picture whose name begins with the /m/ sound.

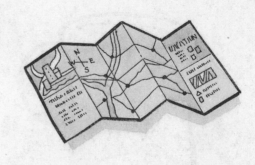

_____   _____
- - - - - - - - - - - - -   - - - - - - - - - - - - -
_____   _____

_____   _____
- - - - - - - - - - - - -   - - - - - - - - - - - - -
_____   _____

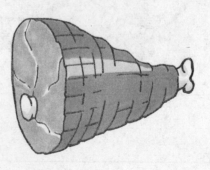

_____   _____
- - - - - - - - - - - - -   - - - - - - - - - - - - -
_____   _____

Directions: Write the capital letter *M* under each picture whose name begins with the /m/ sound.
Write the lowercase letter *m* under each picture whose name ends with the /m/ sound.

Alphabetic Principle • *Skills Practice*

_____

- - - - - - - - - - - - - - - - -

_____

_____

- - - - - - - - - - - - - - - - -

_____

_____

- - - - - - - - - - - - - - - - -

_____

_____

- - - - - - - - - - - - - - - - -

_____

Directions: Write the letter *m* under the picture if it begins with the /m/ sound. Write the letter *s* under the picture if it begins with the /s/ sound.

_____

_____

- - - - - - - - - - - - - - - -

- - - - - - - - - - - - - - - -

_____

_____

_____

_____

- - - - - - - - - - - - - - - -

- - - - - - - - - - - - - - - -

_____

_____

Directions: Write the letter *m* under the picture if it begins with the /m/ sound. Write the letter s under the picture if it begins with the /s/ sound.

Penmanship • *Skills Practice*

Dd

D -

d -

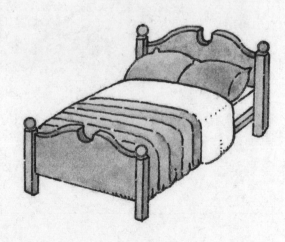

_____   _____

- - - - - - - - - - - - - -   - - - - - - - - - - - - - -
_____   _____

Directions: Write the capital and lowercase forms of the letter *Dd*.
Write the letter *d* under the picture whose name begins with the /d/ sound.

_____

- - - - - - - - - - - - - -

_____

_____

- - - - - - - - - - - - - -

_____

Directions: Write the letter *d* under each picture whose name begins with the /d/ sound.

Penmanship • *Skills Practice*

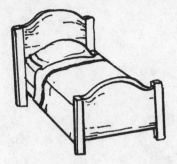

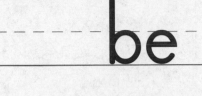
be

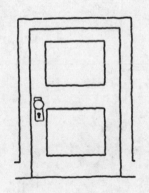

han

oor

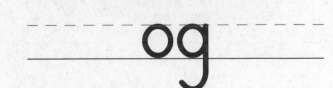
og

Directions: Listen as I say each picture name. Write a *d* to complete each word.

Name _____ **Date** _____

P -

p -

_____   _____

- - - - - - - - - - - - - -   - - - - - - - - - - - - - -

_____   _____

Directions: Write the capital and lowercase forms of the letter *Pp*. Write the letter *p* under the picture whose name begins with the /p/ sound.

Penmanship • *Skills Practice*

_____

- - - - - - - - - - - - - - - -

_____

_____

- - - - - - - - - - - - - - - -

_____

_____

- - - - - - - - - - - - - - - -

_____

_____

- - - - - - - - - - - - - - - -

_____

Directions: Write the letter *p* under each picture whose name begins with the /p/ sound.

_____

- - - - - - - - - - - - - - -

_____

_____

- - - - - - - - - - - - - - -

_____

_____

- - - - - - - - - - - - - - -

_____

_____

- - - - - - - - - - - - - - -

_____

_____

- - - - - - - - - - - - - - -

_____

_____

- - - - - - - - - - - - - - -

_____

Directions: Write the letter *p* under each picture whose name ends with the /p/ sound.

ail

aint

rum

Directions: Listen as I say each picture name. Write a *d* or *p* to complete each word.

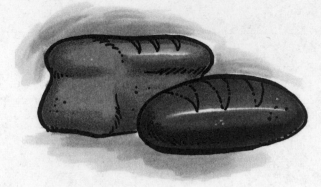

brea

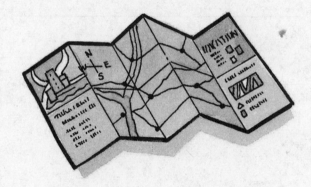

ma

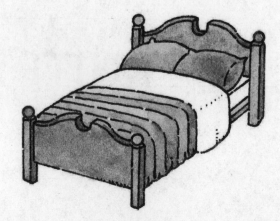

be

Directions: Listen as I say each picture name. Write a *d* or *p* to complete each word.

Penmanship • *Skills Practice*

Name _____ **Date** _____

A ─────────────────────────────

a ─────────────────────────────

─────────────────   ─────────────────

Directions: Write the capital and lowercase forms of the letter *Aa*. Write the letter *a* under the picture whose name has the /a/ sound.

_____

- - - - - - - - - - - -

_____

_____

- - - - - - - - - - - -

_____

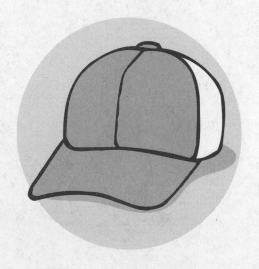

_____

- - - - - - - - - - - -

_____

_____

- - - - - - - - - - - -

_____

Directions: Write the letter a under each picture whose name has the /a/ sound.

Alphabetic Principle • *Skills Practice*

bat

_____

- - - - - - - - - - - - - -

_____

bag

_____

- - - - - - - - - - - - - -

_____

man

_____

- - - - - - - - - - - - - -

_____

pan

_____

- - - - - - - - - - - - - -

_____

Directions: Listen as I say each picture name. Write s, *m*, or *a* if the word has the /s/, /m/, or /a/ sound.

can

_____

- - - - - - - - - - - - - - -

_____

sun

_____

- - - - - - - - - - - - - - -

_____

mug

_____

- - - - - - - - - - - - - - -

_____

hat

_____

- - - - - - - - - - - - - - -

_____

Directions: Listen as I say each picture name. Write s, m, or a if the word has the /s/, /m/, or /a/ sound.

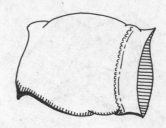

Copyright © McGraw-Hill Education

Directions: Draw a line between the two pictures whose names begin with the /d/ sound. Draw a line between the two pictures whose names begin with the /p/ sound. Draw a line between the two pictures whose names begin with the /a/ sound.

Directions: Listen as I say each picture name. Write the letter that begins each word. Write an *a* next to the other letter if the word has the /a/ sound.

_____

- - - - - - - - - - - - - -

_____

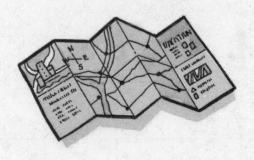

_____

- - - - - - - - - - - - - -

_____

_____

- - - - - - - - - - - - - -

_____

Directions: Listen as I say each picture name. Write the letter that ends each word.

H

h

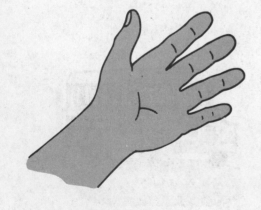

Directions: Write the capital and lowercase forms of the letter *Hh*. Write the letter *h* under the picture whose name begins with the /h/ sound.

Penmanship • *Skills Practice*

_____

- - - - - - - - - - - - - - - - -

_____

_____

- - - - - - - - - - - - - - - - -

_____

_____

- - - - - - - - - - - - - - - - -

_____

_____

- - - - - - - - - - - - - - - - -

_____

Directions: Write the letter *h* under each picture whose name begins with the /h/ sound.

T

t

_____

_____

Directions: Write the capital and lowercase forms of the letter *Tt*. Write the letter *t* under
the picture whose name begins with the /t/ sound.

_____
- - - - - - - - - - - - - - - - -
_____

_____
- - - - - - - - - - - - - - - - -
_____

Directions: Write the letter _t_ under each picture whose name begins with the /t/ sound.

T t

T _____

t _____

_____   _____

- - - - - - - - - - -   - - - - - - - - - - -

_____   _____

Directions: Write the capital and lowercase forms of the letter Tt.
Write the letter t under the picture whose name ends with the /t/ sound.

_____

- -

_____

_____

- -

_____

Directions: Write the letter *t* under each picture whose name ends with the /t/ sound.

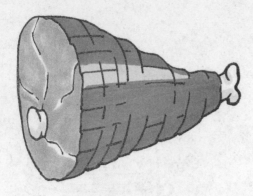

_____

- - - - - - - - am - - - - - - - - -

_____

_____

- - - - - - - - op - - - - - - - - -

_____

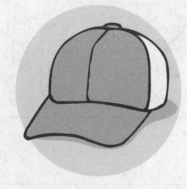

_____

- - - - - - - - at - - - - - - - - -

_____

Directions: Listen as I say each picture name. Write an *h* or a *t* to complete each word.

Penmanship • *Skills Practice*

_____
____ ug ____
_____

10

_____
____ en ____
_____

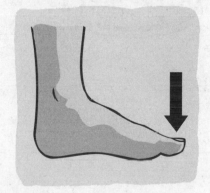

_____
____ oe ____
_____

Directions: Listen as I say each picture name. Write an *h* or a *t* to complete each word.

Nn

N _____

n _____

_____

_____

Directions: Write the capital and lowercase forms of the letter *Nn*.
Write the letter *n* under the picture whose name begins with the
/n/ sound.

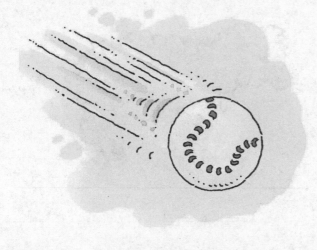

_____

- - - - - - - - - - - - - - - -

_____

_____

- - - - - - - - - - - - - - - -

_____

_____

- - - - - - - - - - - - - - - -

_____

_____

- - - - - - - - - - - - - - - -

_____

Directions: Write the letter *n* under each picture whose name begins with the /n/ sound.

_____

- - - - - - - - - - - - - - -

_____

_____

- - - - - - - - - - - - - - -

_____

_____

- - - - - - - - - - - - - - -

_____

Directions: Write the letter *n* under each picture whose name ends with the /n/ sound.

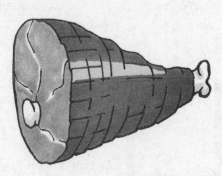

_____

- - - - - - - - - - - - - - -

_____

_____

- - - - - - - - - - - - - - -

_____

_____

- - - - - - - - - - - - - - -

_____

_____

- - - - - - - - - - - - - - -

_____

_____

- - - - - - - - - - - - - - -

_____

_____

- - - - - - - - - - - - - - -

_____

Directions: Write the letter _n_ under each picture whose name ends with the /n/ sound.

L

l

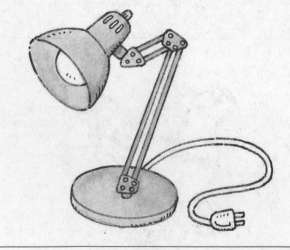

Directions: Write the capital and lowercase forms of the letter *Ll*. Write the letter *l* under the picture whose name begins with the /l/ sound.

Directions: Write the letter *l* under each picture whose name begins with the /l/ sound.

L

Directions: Draw a circle around each object in the picture whose name ends with the /l/ sound. Write the capital form of the letter *Ll*.

Name _____ **Date** _____

Directions: Draw a circle around each object in the picture whose name ends with the /l/ sound. Write the lowercase form of the letter *Ll*.

_____

- - - - - - - ails - - - - - - -

_____

_____

- - - - - - - et - - - - - - -

_____

_____

- - - - - - - ock - - - - - - -

_____

Directions: Listen as I say each picture name. Write an *n* or an *l* to complete each word.

pai

10

te

fa

Directions: Listen as I say each picture name. Write an *n* or an *l* to complete each word.

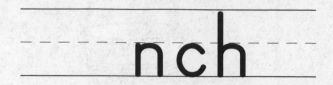

_____ nch _____

_____ nsect

_____ nfant

Directions: Listen as I say each picture name. Write the missing letter *i* to complete each word.

Penmanship • *Skills Practice*

Name _____ **Date** _____

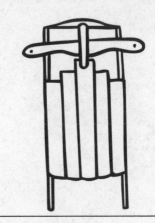

Directions: Listen carefully as I name each picture. Write the letter *i* under the picture if you hear the /i/ sound.

Skills Practice • Alphabetic Principle

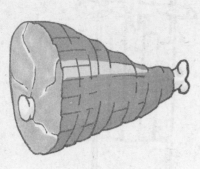

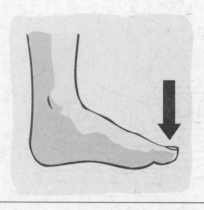

Directions: Listen carefully as I name each picture. Write *h* or *t* under each picture whose name begins with the /h/ or /t/ sound. Write *i* beside the other letter if you hear the /i/ sound.

Directions: Listen carefully as I name each picture. Write the letter *n* under the pictures whose names begin with the /n/ sound. Write the letter *l* under the pictures whose names begin with the /l/ sound. Write *i* beside the other letter if you hear the /i/ sound.

_____   _____

- - - - - - - - - - - - - - - - - -   - - - - - - - - - - - - - - - - - -

_____   _____

_____   _____

- - - - - - - - - - - - - - - - - -   - - - - - - - - - - - - - - - - - -

_____   _____

_____   _____

- - - - - - - - - - - - - - - - - -   - - - - - - - - - - - - - - - - - -

_____   _____

Directions: Listen carefully as I name each picture. Write *h, t, n,* or *l* under each picture whose name begins with the /h/, /t/, /n/, or /l/ sound. Write i beside the other letter if you hear the /i/ sound.

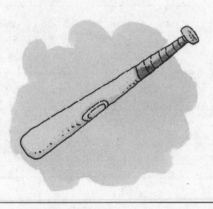

_____

- - - - - - - - - - - - - - - - -

_____

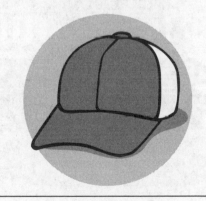

_____

- - - - - - - - - - - - - - - - -

_____

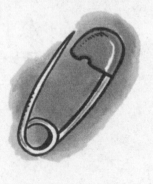

_____

- - - - - - - - - - - - - - - - -

_____

Directions: Listen carefully as I name each picture. Write *t, n,* or *l* under each picture whose name ends with the /t/, /n/, or /l/ sound. Write *i* beside the other letter if you hear the /i/ sound.

Bb

B

b

_____
- - - - - - - - - - - - - - -
_____

_____
- - - - - - - - - - - - - - -
_____

Directions: Write the capital and lowercase forms of the letter *Bb*. Write the letter *b* under the picture whose name begins with the /b/ sound.

_____

- - - - - - - - - - - - - - -

_____

_____

- - - - - - - - - - - - - - -

_____

Directions: Write the letter *b* under each picture whose name begins with the /b/ sound.

_____

- - - - - - - - - - - - - - - - -

_____

_____

- - - - - - - - - - - - - - - - -

_____

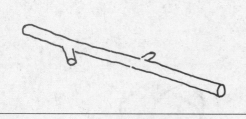

_____

- - - - - - - - - - - - - - - - -

_____

_____

- - - - - - - - - - - - - - - - -

_____

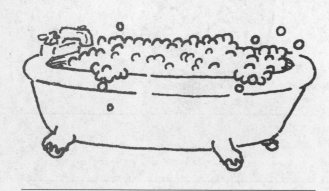

_____

- - - - - - - - - - - - - - - - -

_____

_____

- - - - - - - - - - - - - - - - -

_____

Directions: Write the letter _b_ under each picture whose name ends with the /b/ sound.

C

C

Directions: Write the capital and lowercase forms of the letter *Cc*. Write the letter *c* under the picture whose name begins with the /k/ sound.

_____

- - - - - - - - - - - - - - - - -

_____

_____

- - - - - - - - - - - - - - - - -

_____

Directions: Write the letter *c* under each picture whose name begins with the /k/ sound.

Penmanship • *Skills Practice*

_____

- - - - - - - - - - - - - - - - - - - -

_____

_____

- - - - - - - - - - - - - - - - - - - -

_____

_____

- - - - - - - - - - - - - - - - - - - -

_____

Directions: Write the capital and lowercase forms of the letter Cc under each picture whose name begins with the /k/ sound.

Skills Practice • Alphabetic Principle

B

Directions: Circle all pictures whose names end with the /b/ sound. Write the capital form of the letter *Bb* on the line.

Penmanship • *Skills Practice*

b -

Directions: Circle all pictures whose names end with the /b/ sound. Write the lowercase form of the letter *Bb* on the line.

Skills Practice • Penmanship

Directions: Write the capital and lowercase forms of the letter *Oo*. Write the letter *o* under the picture whose name has the /o/ sound.

_____
- - - - - - - - - - -
_____

_____
- - - - - - - - - - -
_____

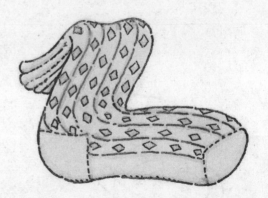

_____
- - - - - - - - - - -
_____

_____
- - - - - - - - - - -
_____

Directions: Write the letter o under each picture whose name has the /o/ sound.

_____

- - - - - - - - - - - - - - - - - - -

_____

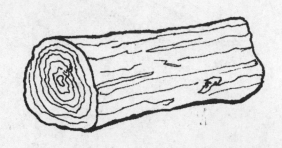

_____

- - - - - - - - - - - - - - - - - - -

_____

_____

- - - - - - - - - - - - - - - - - - -

_____

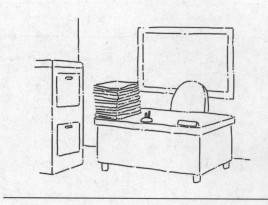

_____

- - - - - - - - - - - - - - - - - - -

_____

_____

- - - - - - - - - - - - - - - - - - -

_____

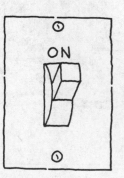

_____

- - - - - - - - - - - - - - - - - - -

_____

Directions: Write the capital form of the letter _O_ under each picture whose name begins with the /o/ sound. Write the lowercase form of the letter _o_ under each picture whose name has the /o/ sound.

Alphabetic Principle • *Skills Practice*

Name _____ **Date** _____

Rr

R _____

r _____

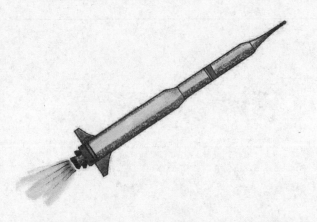

_____   _____

_ _ _ _ _ _ _ _ _ _ _ _   _ _ _ _ _ _ _ _ _ _ _ _

Directions: Write the capital and lowercase forms of the letter *Rr*.
Write the letter *r* under the picture whose name begins with the /r/ sound.

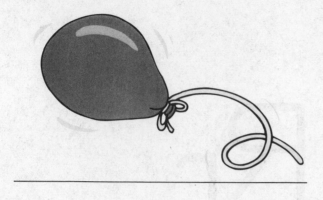

_____

- - - - - - - - - - - - - - - - -

_____

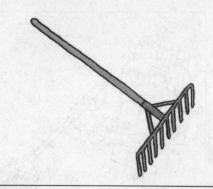

_____

- - - - - - - - - - - - - - - - -

_____

_____

- - - - - - - - - - - - - - - - -

_____

_____

- - - - - - - - - - - - - - - - -

_____

_____

- - - - - - - - - - - - - - - - -

_____

_____

- - - - - - - - - - - - - - - - -

_____

Directions: Write the letter r under each picture whose name begins with the /r/ sound.

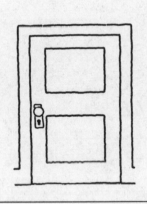

_____

- - - - - - - - - - - - - - - -

_____

_____

- - - - - - - - - - - - - - - -

_____

_____

- - - - - - - - - - - - - - - -

_____

Directions: Write the capital and lowercase forms of the letter *Rr* under each picture whose name
ends with the /r/ sound.

_____

- - - - - - - - - - - - - - -

_____

_____

- - - - - - - - - - - - - - -

_____

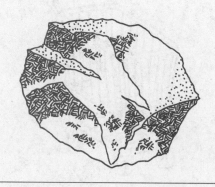

_____

- - - - - - - - - - - - - - -

_____

_____

- - - - - - - - - - - - - - -

_____

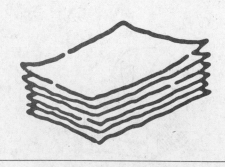

_____

- - - - - - - - - - - - - - -

_____

_____

- - - - - - - - - - - - - - -

_____

Directions: Listen carefully as I name each picture. Write the capital letter *R* under the pictures whose names begin with the /r/ sound. Write the lowercase letter *r* under the pictures whose names end with the /r/ sound. Write the letter *o* beside the other letter if you hear the /o/ sound.

·Penmanship • *Skills Practice*

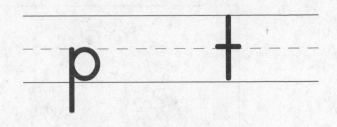

p __ t

sta __

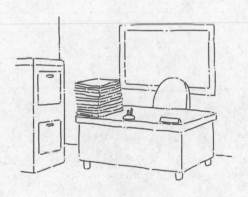

__ ffice

ing

Directions: Listen as I say each picture name. Write an *r* or an *o* to complete each word.

Gg

G

g

Directions: Write the capital and lowercase forms of the letter *Gg*. Write the letter *g* under the picture whose name begins with the /g/ sound.

_____

- - - - - - - - - - - - - - -

_____

_____

- - - - - - - - - - - - - - -

_____

Directions: Write the letter *g* under each picture whose name begins with the /g/ sound.

pig   tag

_____

- - - - - - - - - - -

_____

rug   bug

_____

- - - - - - - - - - -

_____

pig   fig

_____

- - - - - - - - - - -

_____

bag   hug

_____

- - - - - - - - - - -

_____

Directions: Circle the word with the final /g/ sound that names the picture. Then write the letter on each line that makes the /g/ sound.

Alphabetic Principle • *Skills Practice*

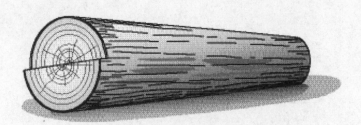

fog   log

_____

- - - - - - - - - - - - - - -

_____

egg   leg

_____

- - - - - - - - - - - - - - -

_____

hog   dog

_____

- - - - - - - - - - - - - - -

_____

bag   wig

_____

- - - - - - - - - - - - - - -

_____

Directions: Circle the word with the final /g/ sound that names the picture. Then write the letter on each line that makes the /g/ sound.

bat   hat

_____

- - - - - - - - - - - - - - -

_____

cat   tot

_____

- - - - - - - - - - - - - - -

_____

bug   dog

_____

- - - - - - - - - - - - - - -

_____

pot   drop

_____

- - - - - - - - - - - - - - -

_____

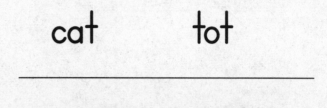
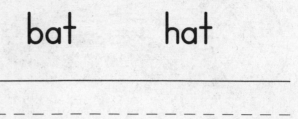

Directions: Circle the word that names the picture. Write the word you circled on the line.

Directions: Write the letter o under each picture whose name has the /o/ sound. Find one
picture name that begins with the /k/ sound and write c under it.

_____

- -

_____

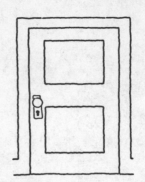

_____

- -

_____

_____

- -

_____

_____

- -

_____

_____

- -

_____

_____

- -

_____

Directions: Listen carefully as I name each picture. Write the letter *o* under each picture whose name has the /o/ sound. Write the letter *r* under the pictures whose names have the /r/ sound. Write the letter *g* if you hear the /g/ sound.

Alphabetic Principle • *Skills Practice*

Jj

J

j

Directions: Write the capital and lowercase forms of the letter *Jj*. Write the letter *j* under the picture whose name begins with the /j/ sound.

_____   _____
- - - - - - - - - - - - - - - -   - - - - - - - - - - - - - - - -
_____   _____

_____   _____
- - - - - - - - - - - - - - - -   - - - - - - - - - - - - - - - -
_____   _____

Directions: Write the letter *j* under each picture whose name begins with the /j/ sound.

F ---

f ---

_____

- -

Directions: Write the capital and lowercase forms of the letter *Ff*. Write the letter *f* under the picture whose name begins with the /f/ sound.

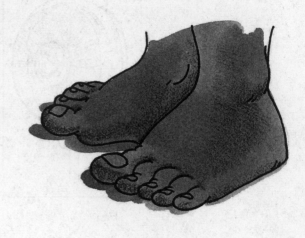

_____

- - - - - - - - - - - - - - - - -

_____

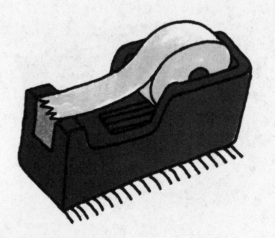

_____

- - - - - - - - - - - - - - - - -

_____

Directions: Write the letter *f* under each picture whose name begins with the /f/ sound.

Penmanship • *Skills Practice*

F ---------------------------------

Directions: Circle the objects in the pictures whose names begin with the /f/ sound. Write the capital form of the letter *Ff* on the line.

Skills Practice • Alphabetic Principle

Directions: Circle the pictures whose names end with the /f/ sound. Write the lowercase form of the letter *Ff* on the line.

Alphabetic Principle • *Skills Practice*

fan   tan

_____

- - - - - - - - - - - - - - -

_____

pump   jump

_____

- - - - - - - - - - - - - - -

_____

hot   jam

_____

- - - - - - - - - - - - - - -

_____

fish   dish

_____

- - - - - - - - - - - - - - -

_____

Directions: Circle the word with the beginning /j/ or /f/ sound that names the picture. Then write the letter on each line that makes the /j/ or /f/ sound.

Uu

U _

u _

_____   _____

_ _ _ _ _ _ _ _ _ _ _ _ _   _ _ _ _ _ _ _ _ _ _ _ _ _

Directions: Write the capital and lowercase forms of the letter *Uu*. Write the letter *u* under the picture whose name has the /u/ sound.

_____   _____
- - - - - - - - - - - - - -   - - - - - - - - - - - - - -
_____   _____

_____   _____
- - - - - - - - - - - - - -   - - - - - - - - - - - - - -
_____   _____

Directions: Write the letter *u* under each picture whose name has the /u/ sound.

Skills Practice • Penmanship

puppy   dog

_____

- - - - - - - - - - - - - - - -

_____

truck   trip

_____

- - - - - - - - - - - - - - - -

_____

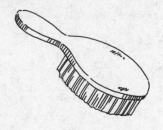

mesh   brush

_____

- - - - - - - - - - - - - - - -

_____

duck   quack

_____

- - - - - - - - - - - - - - - -

_____

Directions: Listen carefully as I say each word. Circle the word with the /u/ sound that names the picture. Then write the capital and lowercase forms of the letter *Uu* on each line.

Alphabetic Principle • *Skills Practice*

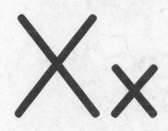

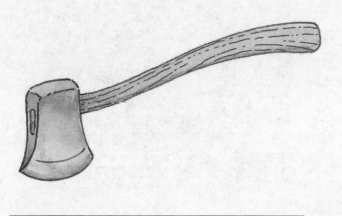

Directions: Write the capital and lowercase forms of the letter *Xx*. Write the letter *x* under the picture whose name ends with the /ks/ sound.

_____

- - - - - - - - - - - - - - - - -

_____

_____

- - - - - - - - - - - - - - - - -

_____

Directions: Write the letter *x* under each picture whose name ends with the /ks/ sound.

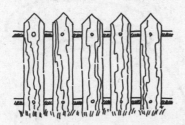

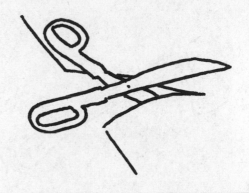

_____

- - - - - - - - - - - - - - - - - -

_____

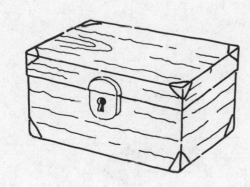

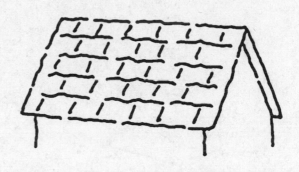

_____

- - - - - - - - - - - - - - - - - -

_____

_____

- - - - - - - - - - - - - - - - - -

_____

Directions: Write the capital and lowercase forms of the letter *Uu* under the pictures whose names have the /u/ sound.

Copyright © McGraw-Hill Education

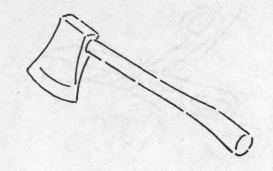

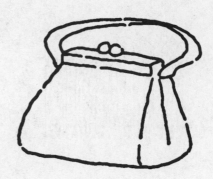

_____

- - - - - - - - - - - - - - - - - -

_____

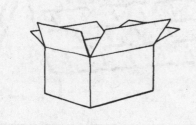

_____

- - - - - - - - - - - - - - - - - -

_____

321
Oak Street

_____

- - - - - - - - - - - - - - - - - -

_____

Directions: Write the capital and lowercase forms of the letter *Xx* under the pictures whose names have the /ks/ sound.

Penmanship • *Skills Practice*

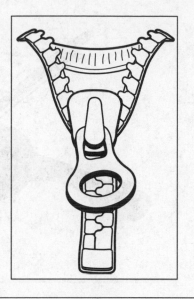

Zz

Z _

z _

Copyright © McGraw-Hill Education

_ _

Directions: Write the capital and lowercase forms of the letter Zz. Write the letter z under the picture whose name begins with the /z/ sound.

_____

- - - - - - - - - - - - - - - - - -

_____

_____

- - - - - - - - - - - - - - - - - -

_____

Directions: Write the letter z under each picture whose name begins with the /z/ sound.

_____

rose

_____

eggs

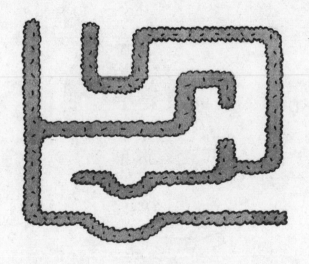

_____

maze

_____

buzz

Directions: Say each picture name. Circle the letter or letters in the name that make the /z/ sound.

prize

nose

fuzz

wigs

Directions: Say each picture name. Circle the letter or letters in the name that make the /z/ sound.

Alphabetic Principle • *Skills Practice*

_____

- - - - - - - - - - - - - - - -

_____

_____

- - - - - - - - - - - - - - - -

_____

_____

- - - - - - - - - - - - - - - -

_____

_____

- - - - - - - - - - - - - - - -

_____

_____

- - - - - - - - - - - - - - - -

_____

_____

- - - - - - - - - - - - - - - -

_____

Directions: Name each picture. Write the letter *j* if the name begins with the /j/ sound. Write the letter *f* if the name begins with the /f/ sound. Write the letter *u* if you hear the /u/ sound.

an

b g

ox

ar

Directions: Listen as I say the name for each picture. Write the missing letter on the line.

Penmanship • *Skills Practice*

Name _____ **Date** _____

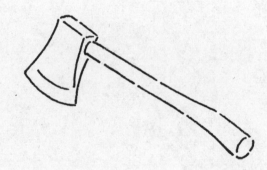

Directions: Listen as I say the name for each picture. Draw a line between the two pictures whose names have the /u/ sound. Draw a line between the two pictures whose names have the /ks/ sound. Draw a line between the two pictures whose names have the /z/ sound.

Skills Practice • Alphabetic Principle

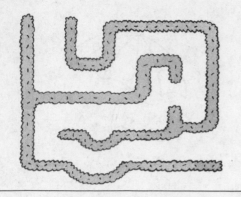

ma _ e

m _ g

_ ork

_ ebra

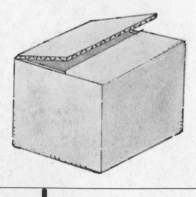

bo _

_ acket

Directions: Listen as I say the name for each picture. Write the missing letter on the line.

W

w

Directions: Write the capital and lowercase forms of the letter *Ww*. Write the letter *w* under the
picture whose name begins with the /w/ sound.

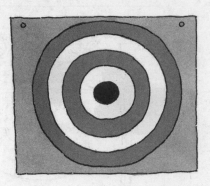

_____

- - - - - - - - - - - - - - - - - -

_____

_____

- - - - - - - - - - - - - - - - - -

_____

Directions: Write the letter *w* under each picture whose name begins with the /w/ sound.

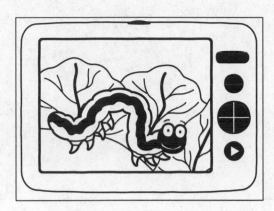

K

K

k

_____

_ _ _ _ _ _ _ _ _ _ _ _ _ _ _ _ _ _ _

_____

Directions: Write the capital and lowercase forms of the letter *Kk*. Write the letter *k* under the picture whose name begins with the /k/ sound.

_____

- - - - - - - - - - - - - - - - - -

_____

_____

- - - - - - - - - - - - - - - - - -

_____

Directions: Write the letter *k* under each picture whose name begins with the /k/ sound.

web   bed

_____

- - - - - - - - - - - - - - -

_____

kite   bike

_____

- - - - - - - - - - - - - - -

_____

yes   keys

_____

- - - - - - - - - - - - - - -

_____

Directions: Circle the word with the /w/ or /k/ sound that names each picture. Then write the letter on each line that makes the /w/ or /k/ sound.

ring   king

_____

- - - - - - - - - - - - - - - -

_____

wig   pig

_____

- - - - - - - - - - - - - - - -

_____

bag   wags

_____

- - - - - - - - - - - - - - - -

_____

Directions: Circle the word with the /w/ or /k/ sound that names each picture. Then write the letter on each line that makes the /w/ or /k/ sound.

Name _____ **Date** _____

E e

E _____

e _____

_____

_____

Directions: Write the capital and lowercase forms of the letter *Ee*. Write the letter *e* under the picture whose name has the /e/ sound.

Skills Practice • Penmanship

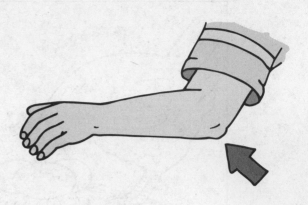

_____   _____

- - - - - - - - - - - - - - - - - -   - - - - - - - - - - - - - - - - - -

_____   _____

_____   _____

- - - - - - - - - - - - - - - - - -   - - - - - - - - - - - - - - - - - -

_____   _____

Directions: Write the letter *e* under each picture whose name begins with the /e/ sound.

Qq

Q

q

Directions: Write the capital and lowercase forms of the letter Qq. Write the letter q under the picture whose name begins with the /kw/ sound.

_____

- - - - - - - - - - - - - - -

_____

_____

- - - - - - - - - - - - - - -

_____

Directions: Write the letter *q* under each picture whose name begins with the /kw/ sound.

elephant   plant

_____

- - - - - - - - - - - - - - -

_____

sack   quack

_____

- - - - - - - - - - - - - - -

_____

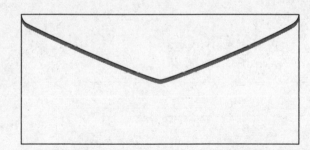

envelope   rope

_____

- - - - - - - - - - - - - - -

_____

Directions: Circle the word with the /e/ or /kw/ sound that names each picture. Then write the letter on each line that makes the /e/ or /kw/ sound.

quilt   built

_____

- - - - - - - - - - - - - - - -

_____

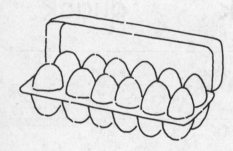

egg   beg

_____

- - - - - - - - - - - - - - - -

_____

kick   quick

_____

- - - - - - - - - - - - - - - -

_____

Directions: Circle the word with the /e/ or /kw/ sound that names each picture. Then write the letter on each line that makes the /e/ or /kw/ sound.

Name _____ **Date** _____

Y — — — — — — — — — — — — — — — — — —

y — — — — — — — — — — — — — — — — — —

— —

Directions: Write the capital and lowercase forms of the letter *Yy*. Write the letter *y* under the picture whose name begins with the /y/ sound.

Skills Practice • Penmanship

V

v

_____

- - - - - - - - - - - -

_____

Directions: Write the capital and lowercase forms of the letter *Vv*. Write the letter *v* under the picture whose name begins with the /v/ sound.

Alphabetic Principle • *Skills Practice*

_____   _____

-    -

_____   _____

_____   _____

-    -

_____   _____

Directions: Write the letter *v* under each picture whose name begins with the /v/ sound.

wagon   bag

_____

- - - - - - - - - - - - - - - -

_____

king   sing

_____

- - - - - - - - - - - - - - - -

_____

wave   move

_____

- - - - - - - - - - - - - - - -

_____

Directions: Circle the word that names the picture. Then write the letter on each line that makes the /w/ or /k/ sound.

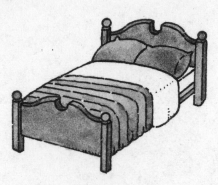

_____

- - - - - - - - - - - -

_____

- - - - - - - - - - - -

_____

_____

- - - - - - - - - - - -

_____

Directions: Write the letter e under each picture whose name has the /e/ sound.

Skills Practice • Penmanship

_____

- - - - - - - - - - - - - - - -

_____

_____

- - - - - - - - - - - - - - - -

_____

Directions: Write the letter *y* under each picture whose name begins with the /y/ sound.

Alphabetic Principle • *Skills Practice*

Zero 0

O   O   O   O   O   O

zero zero zero zero

Directions: Trace the *0*s on the first line. Write a row of *0*s on the second line. Trace the word *zero* on the third line. Practice writing the word *zero* on the fourth line.

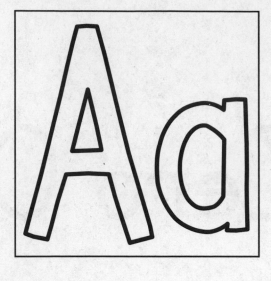 

A

a

Directions: Write the capital and lowercase forms of the letter Aa. Write the letter a under the picture whose name has the /ā/ sound.

One I

I I I I I I I I I I

one one one one one

Directions: Trace the *1s* on the first line. Write a row of *1s* on the second line. Trace the word *one* on the third line. Practice writing the word *one* on the fourth line.

_____   _____
- - - - - - - - - - - - - - - - - -   - - - - - - - - - - - - - - - - - -
_____   _____

_____   _____
- - - - - - - - - - - - - - - - - -   - - - - - - - - - - - - - - - - - -
_____   _____

Directions: Write the letter *a* under each picture whose name has the /ā/ sound.

O ‒ ‒ ‒ ‒ ‒ ‒ ‒ ‒ ‒ ‒ ‒ ‒ ‒ ‒ ‒ ‒ ‒ ‒

I ‒ ‒ ‒ ‒ ‒ ‒ ‒ ‒ ‒ ‒ ‒ ‒ ‒ ‒ ‒ ‒ ‒ ‒

‒ ‒ ‒ ‒ ‒ ‒ ‒ ‒ ‒ ‒   ‒ ‒ ‒ ‒ ‒ ‒ ‒ ‒ ‒ ‒

Directions: Write the numbers *0* and *1* on the lines. Count the number of apples in each tree and write the correct number on the line.

Two 2

2 2 2 2 2 2 2 2

two two two two two

Directions: Trace the 2s on the first line. Write a row of 2s in the second line. Trace the word *two* on the third line. Practice writing the word *two* on the fourth line.

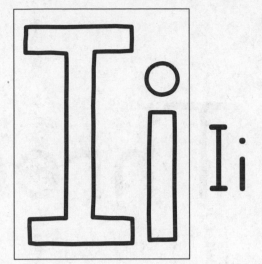

I

- -

i

- -

_____

- -

_____

Directions: Write the capital and lowercase forms of the letter *Ii*. Write the letter *i* under the picture whose name has the /ī/ sound.

Three 3

3 3 3 3 3 3 3

three three three three

Copyright © McGraw-Hill Education

Directions: Trace the *3s* on the first line. Write a row of *3s* in the second line. Trace the word *three* on the third line. Practice writing the word *three* on the fourth line.

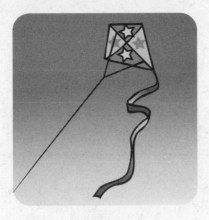

_____

- - - - - - - - - - - - - - - - - -

_____

_____

- - - - - - - - - - - - - - - - - -

_____

Directions: Write the letter *i* under each picture whose name has the /ī/ sound.

Skills Practice • Alphabetic Principle

2

3

Directions: Write the numbers 2 and 3 on the lines. Count the number of apples in each tree and write the correct number on the line.

Penmanship • *Skills Practice*

Four 4

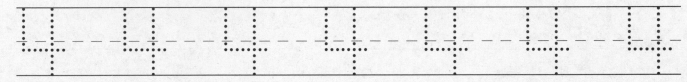

four four four four four four

Directions: Trace the *4*s on the first line. Write a row of *4*s on the second line. Trace the word
four on the third line. Practice writing the word *four* on the fourth line.

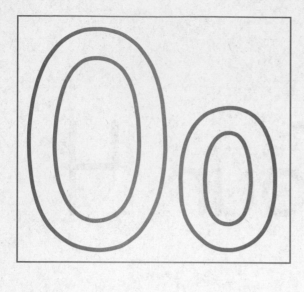

Directions: Write the capital and lowercase forms of the letter *Oo*. Write the letter *o* under the picture whose name has the /ō/ sound in it.

Penmanship • *Skills Practice*

Five 5

5 5 5 5 5 5 5

five five five five five

Directions: Trace the 5s on the first line. Write a row of 5s on the second line. Trace the word *five* on the third line. Practice writing the word *five* on the fourth line.

_____

- -

_____

_____

- -

_____

Directions: Write the letter *o* under each picture whose name has the /ō/ sound.

4 ----------------------------------

5 - - - - - - - - - - - - - - - - - -

_____   _____

- - - - - - - - - - - -   - - - - - - - - - - - -

_____   _____

Directions: Write the numbers 4 and 5 on the lines. Count the number of apples in each tree and write the correct number on the line.

six 6

6 6 6 6 6 6 6

six six six six six six

Directions: Trace the 6s on the first line. Write a row of 6s on the second line. Trace the word *six* on the third line. Practice writing the word *six* on the fourth line.

Name _____ **Date** _____

U u

Directions: Write the capital and lowercase forms of the letter *Uu*. Write the letter *u* under the picture whose name has the /ū/ sound in it.

Skills Practice • Alphabetic Principle

seven 7

7 7 7 7 7 7 7 7 7

seven seven seven

Directions: Trace the 7s on the first line. Write a row of 7s on the second line. Trace the word *seven* on the third line. Practice writing the word *seven* on the fourth line.

Penmanship • *Skills Practice*

_____

- - - - - - - - - - - - - - - - - -

_____

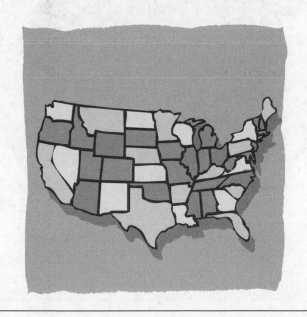

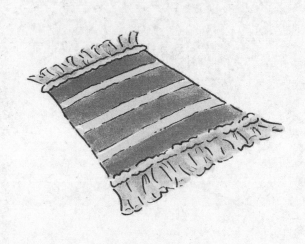

_____

- - - - - - - - - - - - - - - - - -

_____

Directions: Write the letter *u* under each picture whose name has the /ū/ sound in it.

6 -

7 -

_____   _____

- - - - - - - - - - - -   - - - - - - - - - - - -

_____   _____

Directions: Write the numbers 6 and 7 on the lines. Count the
number of apples in each tree and write the correct number on the line.

eight 8

8 8 8 8 8 8 8

_____

_ _ _ _ _ _ _ _ _ _ _ _ _ _ _ _ _ _ _

eight eight eight eight

_____

_ _ _ _ _ _ _ _ _ _ _ _ _ _ _ _ _ _ _

Directions: Trace the *8s* on the first line. Write a row of *8s* on the second line. Trace the word *eight* on the third line. Practice writing the word *eight* on the fourth line.

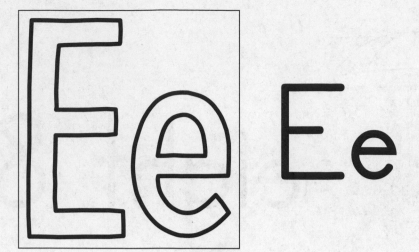

E -

e -

_____   _____
- - - - - - - - - - - - - - - - -   - - - - - - - - - - - - - - - - -
_____   _____

Directions: Write the capital and lowercase forms of the letter *Ee.* Write the letter *e* under the
picture whose name has the /ē/ sound in it.

_____

- - - - - - - - - - - - - - - - - -

_____

_____

- - - - - - - - - - - - - - - - - -

_____

Directions: Write the letter e under each picture whose name has the /ē/ sound.

Skills Practice • Alphabetic Principle

nine 9

9 9 9 9 9 9 9

nine nine nine nine

Directions: Trace the 9s on the first line. Write a row of 9s on the second line. Trace the word *nine* on the third line. Practice writing the word *nine* on the fourth line.

_____
- - - - - - - - - - - - - - - - - -
_____

_____
- - - - - - - - - - - - - - - - - -
_____

Directions: Write the letter e under the picture whose name begins with the /ē/ sound.

Ee

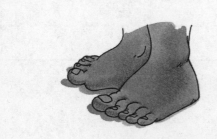

Ee

Directions: Write the letter e under each picture whose name has the /ē/ sound in the middle sound.

8

9

Directions: Write the numbers 8 and 9 on the lines. Count the number of apples in each tree and write the correct number on the line.

_____

- - - - - - - - - - - - - - - -

_____

_____

- - - - - - - - - - - - - - - -

_____

_____

- - - - - - - - - - - - - - - -

_____

Directions: Write the capital *A* under each picture whose name has the /ā/ sound.
Write a lowercase *a* under each picture whose name has the /a/ sound.

ten 10

10 10 10 10 10 10

_____

_ _ _ _ _ _ _ _ _ _ _ _ _ _ _ _ _ _

_____

ten ten ten ten ten ten

_____

_ _ _ _ _ _ _ _ _ _ _ _ _ _ _ _ _ _

_____

Directions: Trace the *10s* on the first line. Write a row of *10s* on the second line. Trace the word *ten* on the third line. Practice writing the word *ten* on the fourth line.

Directions: Write the capital *I* under each picture whose name has the /ī/ sound. Write a
lowercase *i* under each picture whose name has the /i/ sound.

168 UNIT 9 • Lesson 3 • Day 2   Alphabetic Principle • *Skills Practice*

_____

- - - - - - - - - - - - - - - - - -

_____

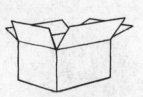

_____

- - - - - - - - - - - - - - - - - -

_____

_____

- - - - - - - - - - - - - - - - - -

_____

Directions: Write the capital *O* under each picture whose name has the /ō/ sound. Write a lowercase *o* under each picture whose name has the /o/ sound.

Skills Practice • Alphabetic Principle   UNIT 9 • Lesson 3 • Day 3   **169**

0 zero	1 one	2 two
3 three	4 four	5 five

2 two

Directions: Look at each picture and count the apples. Write the number of apples on the line. Then write the name of the number.

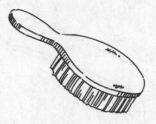

_____

- - - - - - - - - - - - - - - - -

_____

_____

- - - - - - - - - - - - - - - - -

_____

_____

- - - - - - - - - - - - - - - - -

_____

Directions: Write the capital *U* under each picture whose name has the /ū/ sound. Write a lowercase *u* under each picture whose name has the /u/ sound.

Skills Practice • Alphabetic Principle

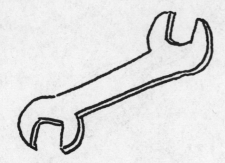

Directions: Write the capital *E* under each picture whose name has the /ē/ sound. Write a lowercase *e* under each picture whose name has the /e/ sound.

Alphabetic Principle • *Skills Practice*

6 six	7 seven	8 eight
9 nine	10 ten	

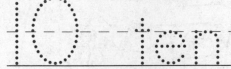

10 ten

Copyright © McGraw-Hill Education

Directions: Look at each picture and count the apples. Write the number of apples on the line.
Then write the name of the number.

Skills Practice • Alphabetic Principle   UNIT 9 • Lesson 3 • Day 5 **173**

1. Sam _____ on a rock.

   hat   sat

2. Where is the _____?

   map   lap

3. The letter needs a _____.

   stamp   lamp

4. Wipe your shoes on the _____.

   mat   pat

Directions: Listen as I read each sentence. Look at the picture. Blend and read
each word. Circle the best word to fill the blank and then write the word on the line.

1. The beaver built a _____.

   dam   ham

2. Maya feels _____ today.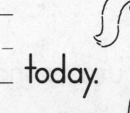

   said   sad

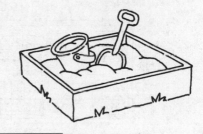

3. Can we play in the _____?

   sand   land

4. The dog's fur was _____.

   damp   dame

Directions: Listen as I read each sentence. Look at the picture. Blend and read each word. Circle the best word to fill the blank and then write the word on the line.

1. Do not eat the peach _____.

   hit   pit

2. His drum is made of _____.

   tin   tint

3. _____ the note to the board.

   Pin   Pan

4. One _____ is on the cone.

   rip   dip

Directions: Listen as I read each sentence. Look at the picture. Blend and read each word. Circle the best word to fill the blank and then write the word on the line.

1. Rosa's hair is in a _____.

    bun   bin

2. A baby bear is a _____?

    cab   cub

3. An acorn is a _____.

    nut   rut

4. Did you _____ the paper?

    cut   curt

Copyright © McGraw-Hill Education

Directions: Listen as I read each sentence. Look at the picture. Blend and read each word. Circle the best word to fill the blank and then write the word on the line.

1. Do not _____ about your doll.

   big   brag

2. Here is my school _____?

   bag   rag

3. Is that a mouse or a _____?

   rat   rap

4. The shirt has a _____.

   tab   tag

Directions: Listen as I read each sentence. Look at the picture. Blend and read each word. Circle the best word to fill the blank and then write the word on the line.

Phonics • *Skills Practice*

1. The clown wore a _____.

wag   wig

2. Do the shoes _____?

fit   lit

3. See the shark's _____.

fin   fan

4. Can you _____ the ball?

hat   hit

Directions: Listen as I read each sentence. Look at the picture. Blend and read each word. Circle the best word to fill the blank and then write the word on the line.

1. Is the apple ___*feb*___?

red   ride

2. Please make the ___*bed*___.

bed   did

3. The dog can ___*beb*___.

bag   beg

4. Lin's ___*pec*___ is a cat.

pat   pet

Directions: Listen as I read each sentence. Look at the picture. Blend and read each word. Circle the best word to fill the blank and then write the word on the line.

Phonics • *Skills Practice*

1. Lisa is very _____.

    hot   hat

2. Can you draw a _____?

    dot   got

3. Fish swim in the _____.

    pen   pond

4. The rabbit can _____.

    hop   hip

Directions: Listen as I read each sentence. Look at the picture. Blend and read each word. Circle the best word to fill the blank and then write the word on the line.

1. _____ the dog gently.

   (pat)   rat

2. The car needs _____.

   gap   (gas)

3. The kids play _____.

   (tag)   (tan)

4. A _____ is a deer.

   (stag)   star

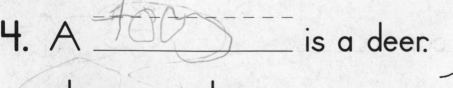

Directions: Listen as I read each sentence. Look at the picture. Blend and read each word. Circle the best word to fill the blank and then write the word on the line.

1. Those stores ___sell___ shoes.

(sell)   shell

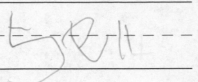

2. The circus had two ___tents___?

tans   (tents)

3. Use ___nets___ to catch the fish.

(nets)   nuts

4. The _____ lay eggs.

hens   hands

Directions: Listen as I read each sentence. Look at the picture. Blend and read each word. Circle the best word to fill the blank and then write the word on the line.

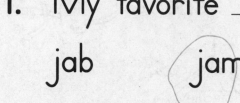
1. My favorite 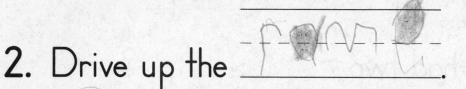 is grape.

jab   (jam)

2. Drive up the _____.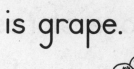

(ramp)   (map)

3. I saw a _____ at the zoo.

ham   (ram)

4. Leo likes 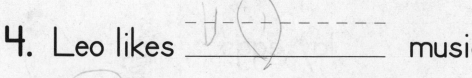 music.

(rap)   rip

Directions: Listen as I read each sentence. Look at the picture. Blend and read each word. Circle the best word to fill the blank and then write the word on the line.

1. Sam wore a _____.

   nest   vest

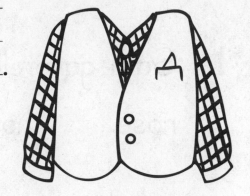

2. _____ are animal doctors.

   vets   vats

3. Where are the butterfly _____?

   nets   bets

4. Bears live in _____.

   dent   dens

Directions: Listen as I read each sentence. Look at the picture. Blend and read each word. Circle the best word to fill the blank and then write the word on the line.

Name _____ **Date** _____

1. Sam gave Jill a __rose__.

   rose   hose

2. Where is the __rope__?

   hope   rope

3. Meg __rode__ a horse.

   rode   code

4. Joe __mops__ the floor each day.

   hops   mops

Directions: Listen as I read each sentence. Look at the picture. Blend and read each word. Circle the best word to fill the blank and then write the word on the line.

Phonics • *Skills Practice*

1. _____ comes from trees.

   sat   sap

2. They held books in their _____?

   maps   laps

3. Boys are also called _____.

   lads   labs

4. Football players wear _____.

   pills   pads

Directions: Listen as I read each sentence. Look at the picture. Blend and read each word. Circle the best word to fill the blank and then write the word on the line.

1. One _____ of the box is open.

   hide   side

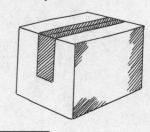

2. Are any birds in the _____?

   nest   rest

3. We can _____ in the pool.

   swim   swam

4. That cap is _____.

   line   mine

Directions: Listen as I read each sentence. Look at the picture. Blend and read each word. Circle the best word to fill the blank and then write the word on the line.

1. June landed on the _____.

   hat   mat

2. The car has new _____.

   mats   math

3. The dog _____ on the floor.

   sit   sat

4. I _____ dinner.

   late   ate

Directions: Listen as I read each sentence. Look at the picture. Blend and read each word. Circle the best word to fill the blank and then write the word on the line.

1. Lee feels _____ today.

    mad   made

2. Beavers build _____.

    dim   dams

3. These ducks look the _____.

    same   some

4. The trainer _____ lions.

    tame   tames

Directions: Listen as I read each sentence. Look at the picture. Blend and read each word. Circle the best word to fill the blank and then write the word on the line.

1. Sailboats have _____.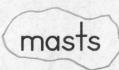

   (masts)   mask

2. The letter needs more _____.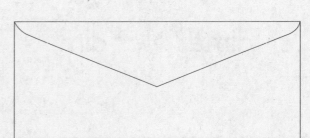

   stumps   (stamps)

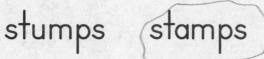

3. _____ is a kind of glue.

   (paste)   waste

4. Can you label the _____?

   skates   states

Directions: Listen as I read each sentence. Look at the picture. Blend and read each word. Circle the best word to fill the blank and then write the word on the line.

1. Do not ___rip___ your pants.

trip   (rip)

2. Tim put a ___dime___ in his bank.

(dime)   dim

3. What ___time___ is it?

(time)   lime

4. Sam wore football ___pads___.

pad   (pads)

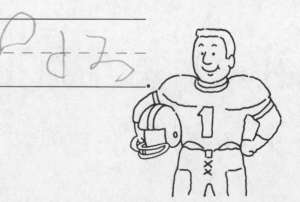

Directions: Listen as I read each sentence. Look at the picture. Blend and read each word. Circle the best word to fill the blank and then write the word on the line.

1. Jan uses _____ in art class.

   past   paste

2. The ticket cost a _____.

   dime   time

3. Jason feels _____ tonight.

   said   sad

4. Did you _____ the cake?

   bake   rake

Directions: Listen as I read each sentence. Look at the picture. Blend and read each word. Circle the best word to fill the blank and then write the word on the line.

1. __Stop__ your car at the sign.

   (stop)   top

2. Aim between the goal __posts__.

   most   (posts)

3. Sasha __mopes__ around the house.

   (mopes)   (maps)

4. Carlos __totes__ books in his bag.

   toots   (totes)

Directions: Listen as I read each sentence. Look at the picture. Blend and read each word. Circle the best word to fill the blank and then write the word on the line.

1. The duck is on his _____.

 nest   rest

2. Where are the butterfly _____?

nuts   nets

3. Do not _____ in the puddle.

 step   steep

4. _____ beating that drum!

 stop   top

Directions: Listen as I read each sentence. Look at the picture. Blend and read each word. Circle the best word to fill the blank and then write the word on the line.

Skills Practice • Phonics

1. Joe has __lots__ of pet fish.

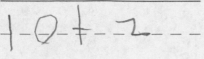

 ~~lots~~   dots

2. The kitten is __lost__.

list   ~~lost~~

3. The ice will __melt__.

~~melt~~   meet

4. I __sold__ cookies at the bake sale.

mold   ~~sold~~

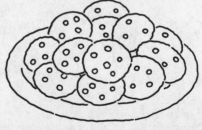

Directions: Listen as I read each sentence. Look at the picture. Blend and read each word. Circle the best word to fill the blank and then write the word on the line.

Name _____ **Date** _____

1. Smell the red _____.
   rode   rose

2. I watched the sun _____.
   rise   prize

3. Can you _____ a bicycle?
   ride   side

4. Dad's car has a flat _____.
   tired   tire

Directions: Listen as I read each sentence. Look at the picture. Blend and read each word. Circle the best word to fill the blank and then write the word on the line.

Skills Practice • Phonics   UNIT 11 • Lesson 2 • Day 4   **197**

1. Please _____ the door.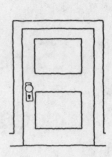

   open   opens

2. Lola always said no or _____.

   mope   nope

3. Can you untie the _____?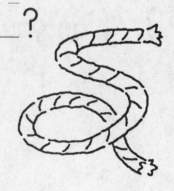

   rope   ripe

4. We need _____ bananas.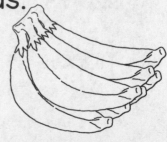

   move   more

Directions: Listen as I read each sentence. Look at the picture. Blend and read each word. Circle the best word to fill the blank and then write the word on the line.

1. Sam _____ the dirty floor.

   mops   maps

2. The hare _____ quickly.

   tops   hops

3. Many chefs wear _____.

   hats   hits

4. Pat _____ around the house.

   mopes   hopes

Directions: Listen as I read each sentence. Look at the picture. Blend and read each word. Circle the best word to fill the blank and then write the word on the line.

1. His eyes were _____ of coal.

    fits   bits

2. The chipmunk _____ the nut.

    boots   bites

3. Where does the cat _____?

    hide   hid

4. Glen needs a _____.

    hint   dent

Directions: Listen as I read each sentence. Look at the picture. Blend and read each word. Circle the best word to fill the blank and then write the word on the line.

1. The _____ was sharp.

    ax   back

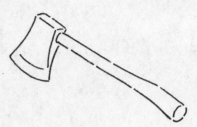

2. An _____ lives on the farm.

    locks   ox

3. Do you like chocolate _____?

    cake   kick

4. The clown told a funny_____.

    joke   poke

Directions: Listen as I read each sentence. Look at the picture. Blend and read each word. Circle the best word to fill the blank and then write the word on the line.

1. We need to get _____ of the ants.

   (rid)   hid

2. Amy can _____ 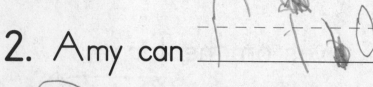 a bicycle.

   (ride)   side

3. _____ the nail with the hammer.

   trap   tap

4. Can I borrow your _____ ?

   (tape)   gape

Directions: Listen as I read each sentence. Look at the picture. Blend and read each word. Circle the best word to fill the blank and then write the word on the line.

1. _____ your nose.

   white   wipe

2. Did Lana _____ the match?

   win   bin

3. I _____ my oatmeal with milk.

   mix   six

4. That ball is _____.

   my   mine

Directions: Listen as I read each sentence. Look at the picture. Blend and read each word. Circle the best word to fill the blank and then write the word on the line.

Name _____ **Date** _____

1. _____

   _____ along the dotted line.

   cat   cut

2. Katie can _____ quickly!

   run   runt

3. Please _____ the bedroom.

   dust   last

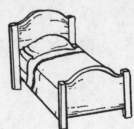

4. We need an air _____.

   lump   pump

Directions: Listen as I read each sentence. Look at the picture. Blend and read each word. Circle the best word to fill the blank and then write the word on the line.

1. Birds _____ their wings to fly.

   use   used

2. Sara will _____ the box.

   ready   reuse

3. Is that your pet _____?

   rule   mule

4. I want one more ice _____.

   cube   tube

Directions: Listen as I read each sentence. Look at the picture. Blend and read each word. Circle the best word to fill the blank and then write the word on the line.

1. We need a _____ of cat food.

    call   case

2. The twins want two _____.

    lake   cakes

3. Here are the ice _____.

    cubes   cubs

4 Did you _____ the cookies?

    back   bake

Directions: Listen as I read each sentence. Look at the picture. Blend and read each
word. Circle the best word to fill the blank and then write the word on the line.

Phonics • *Skills Practice*

1. The dog _____ barking.

   quit   kit

2. The class took a _____.

   queen   quiz

3. A _____ is an ocean creature.

   squid   kid

4. A _____ is a shape.

   square   care

Directions: Listen as I read each sentence. Look at the picture. Blend and read each
word. Circle the best word to fill the blank and then write the word on the line.

1. We drink from _____.

   cups   clips

2. Baby bears are called _____.

   cubs   cud

3. I have three ice _____.

   rubs   cubes

4. The radio plays _____.

   music   muse

Directions: Listen as I read each sentence. Look at the picture. Blend and read each
word. Circle the best word to fill the blank and then write the word on the line.

Name _____ **Date** _____

1. Some apples are _____.

   red   bed

2. Can I borrow your _____?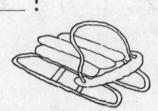

   sled   slid

3. I will fix the _____ fishing rod.

   bit   bent

4. The nail is _____.

   unbent   undo

Directions: Listen as I read each sentence. Look at the picture. Blend and read each
word. Circle the best word to fill the blank and then write the word on the line.

1. The bus is _____.

   there   here

2. Did you enjoy New Year's _____.
   Eve   even

3. I _____ the computer game.

   rest   reset

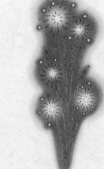

4. Tasha _____ the fabric.

   recut   recall

Directions: Listen as I read each sentence. Look at the picture. Blend and read each word. Circle the best word to fill the blank and then write the word on the line.

Phonics • *Skills Practice*

1. The car needs more _____ .

   has   gas

2. Please _____ more bread.

   get   got

3. I _____ out the window.

   page   gaze

4. She can _____ the shovel.

   regret   regrip

Directions: Listen as I read each sentence. Look at the picture. Blend and read each
word. Circle the best word to fill the blank and then write the word on the line.

1. We ride in the back of the _____.

   van   win

2. The roses need a _____.

   vase   vast

3. I turned _____ today!

   sell   seven

4. Jamal will _____ the bus.

   drive   alive

Directions: Listen as I read each sentence. Look at the picture. Blend and read each word. Circle the best word to fill the blank and then write the word on the line.

1. Fido is my _____ friend.

rest   best

2. Sam _____ Jen a rose.

gave   gale

3. The score is _____ .

even   eve

4. _____ the toaster.

replug   refresh

Directions: Listen as I read each sentence. Look at the picture. Blend and read each
word. Circle the best word to fill the blank and then write the word on the line.

1. Cheetahs are very _____ .
   test   fast

2. This is the fish's dorsal _____ .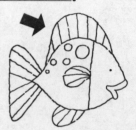
   find   fin

3. Thank you for the _____ !
   gift   give

4. The jewel is _____ .
   take   fake

Directions: Listen as I read each sentence. Look at the picture. Blend and read each word. Circle the best word to fill the blank and then write the word on the line.

1. Tom read about _____.

   yaks   takes

2. The ox wore a _____.

   joke   yoke

3. Dogs sometimes _____.

   yelp   yell

4. I want a _____ with dinner.

   them   yam

Directions: Listen as I read each sentence. Look at the picture. Blend and read each word. Circle the best word to fill the blank and then write the word on the line.

_____

1. Jim likes _____ on toast.

    jam   dam

2. What a pretty _____ ring!

    jade   jet

3. My dog can _____ high.

    lamp   jump

4. Ann likes to _____.

    hog   jog

Directions: Listen as I read each sentence. Look at the picture. Blend and read each word. Circle the best word to fill the blank and then write the word on the line.

Phonics • *Skills Practice*

1. _____ your coat today.

zip   sap

2. The sun _____ in the east.

rode   rose

3. I have two pet _____.

pigs   legs

4. Jose won first _____!

please   prize

Directions: Listen as I read each sentence. Look at the picture. Blend and read each word. Circle the best word to fill the blank and then write the word on the line.

1. Lightning can _____ a pole.

   zap   cup

2. All countries have _____.

   flags   figs

3. The farmer planted _____.

   swims   yams

4. The clown's _____ is round.

   nose   news

Directions: Listen as I read each sentence. Look at the picture. Blend and read each word. Circle the best word to fill the blank and then write the word on the line.